Contemporary Crafts

Rag Rugs

ANN DAVIES

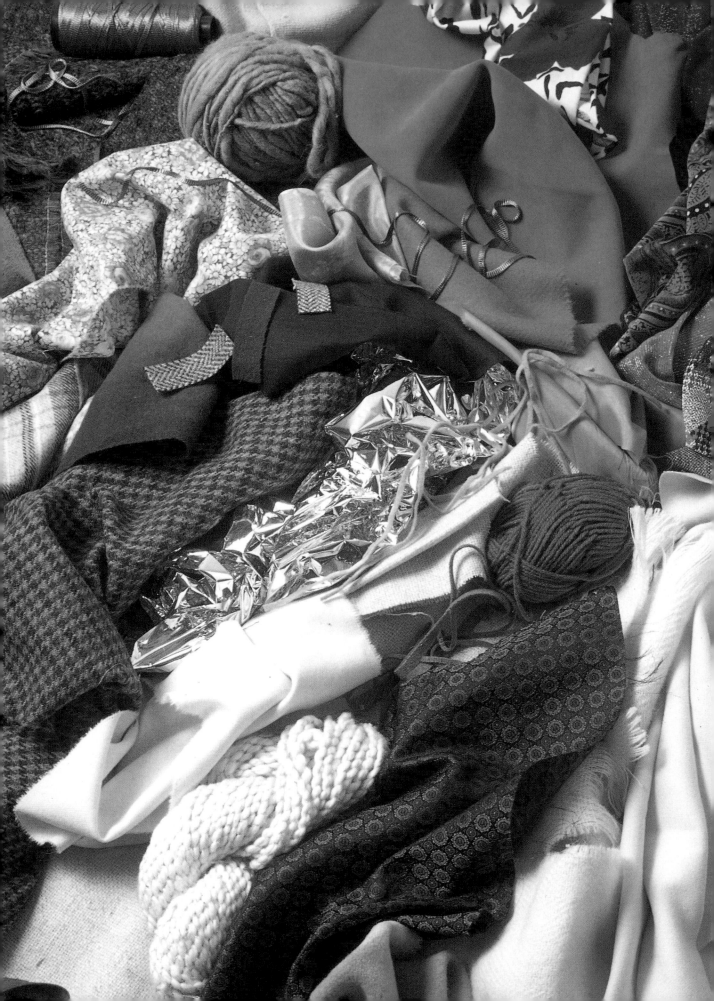

Contemporary Crafts

Rag Rugs

Ann Davies

An Owl Book

HENRY HOLT
AND
COMPANY

NEW YORK

Designed and edited by
Anness Publishing Limited, London

Editorial Director: Joanna Lorenz
Project Editor: Judith Simons
Text Editor: Alison Leach
Design: Millions Design
Photographer: Sue Atkinson
Illustrator: Paula Soper

Printed and bound in Spain by
Printer industria grafica s.a.

1   3   5   7   9   10   8   6   4   2

ACKNOWLEDGEMENTS

Special thanks are due to Jenny Owen for providing examples of traditional rag rugs for photography; John and Heather Richardson, and Chris Gapp for location photography; The Pine Place, St Leonard's Road, Windsor, Berks, for supplying props; Caroline Harris, A. Gran & Co., and Valerie Wolsey for providing scrap materials; and Kirsty Wilson for modelling. The photograph on page 6 is reproduced by permission of The American Museum in Britain, Bath.

CONTENTS

INTRODUCTION   6

MATERIALS AND EQUIPMENT   8

BASIC TECHNIQUES   14

GALLERY   20

PROJECTS

CUSHION COVER   29

RAZZLE DAZZLE   33

GARDEN WALLHANGING   37

'BROKEN GLASS' RUG   43

STAR-BURST RUG   49

LUCKY BLACK CAT   55

EDGE OF THE RIVER   61

BRIGHT AND BREEZY   67

BLOSSOM TIME   73

SHAGGY BLUE RUG   79

'STAINED-GLASS' LANDSCAPE   85

PRODDED DIAMOND RUG   91

SUPPLIERS   95

INDEX   96

INTRODUCTION

RAG RUG-MAKING has been practised in one form or another for centuries, and despite fluctuations in popularity over the years, has proved an enduring and highly accessible folk craft.

The resurgence of interest in rag rug-making today is not only a response to the great variety of creative possibilities in this attractive craft, but also reflects the growing awareness of the need to conserve natural resources. It is essentially a thrift craft, traditionally making use of recycled and scrap materials. The basic requirements of a frame, a hook or prodder, and hessian/burlap are relatively inexpensive. The rug or tapestry canvas used as the base material in some of the more ambitious projects described in this book is more expensive; even so, a hard-wearing and visually appealing rug or wallhanging need not cost a great deal to make.

Of the various types of rag rugs, those made by the hooking and prodding techniques are the most familiar. There are numerous regional variations of these terms, such as hooky, proggy, bodged and clippy. Hooked rugs, as the name implies, are made by pulling long strips of material through from the back of the base material to the front, using a tool very similar to a crochet hook but with a more acute angle, thus producing a looped pile. For prodded rugs, holes are made in the base material

This beautiful American hooked rug features repeated flower panels on a geometric background. Made during the latter part of the 19th century, the design was influenced by quilt patterns of the day.

with a pointed piece of wood or metal; a small piece of material is then pushed through the hole from the back to the front, making a shaggy pile.

The concept of introducing a loop into a base material was probably originated by the Copts in Egypt well over a thousand years ago; the Vikings too used a form of loop in some of their textiles. William Winthrop Kent, an American architect who was fascinated by the examples of rag rug-making he saw in North America in the 1930s, was the first person to study the origins of the craft. His research convinced him that rag rug-making had originated in Europe, and he corresponded extensively with British contacts, notably Ann Macbeth, a contemporary authority on textiles, who had been the chief instructress in the Embroidery Department of the Glasgow School of Art from 1908 to 1920. William Winthrop Kent summed up his research in his book *The Hooked Rug* (long out of print), by concluding that although hooked rugs had been known in Britain since Tudor times, and their origins were indeed European, 'yet it is fact that the art was taken up more widely and developed more artistically in America than elsewhere'. He attributed this to the early settlers including 'both Latins and Irish, instinctively and generally art-loving'. Wherever their birthplaces had been, these American housewives in the main produced rugs that were more decorative than those made in Britain at that time.

The heyday of rag rug-making in the British Isles was in the late 19th and early 20th centuries, when it was an intrinsic part of life for many working-class families. Interest in the craft then diminished, except in areas most affected by the years of the Depression and in the more isolated rural communities. People still make rugs from Scotland to Cornwall, and although it may be popularly considered as being a traditionally North Country craft, in the course of my travels, both teaching and demonstrating, I have met many people who can remember their parents and grandparents making rag rugs in other places as diverse as Wales, Kent, Sussex, East Anglia, Worcestershire and the East End of London. During World War II a wide variety of rag rugs were made all over the United Kingdom as part of the 'Make Do and Mend' campaign.

Unfortunately, however, the craft is not terribly well documented in the United Kingdom, where – especially in Victorian times – it was considered a working-class craft not worthy of attention. Because the base material then used was often loose-meshed sacking, the strips of material had to be cut extremely wide in order to fill in the holes, making the rugs heavy and difficult to clean. They were mostly utilitarian articles with wide black or dark borders, but they were the only form of floor covering the makers could afford. Consequently, rag rug-making was associated with poverty. As people became more affluent, they began to be ashamed of their rag rugs and many of them were thrown away. Some of the most exceptional pieces were preserved and are now held in specialist collections.

Rag rug-making in the United States has always been of the hooked variety, but prodded rugs, known as poked mats, were made in both Canada and Newfoundland. Many people associate the craft primarily with the eastern seaboard of the North American continent, particularly in Maine, the Maritime Provinces of Canada and Newfoundland, where it is still a rural industry. Today there is also a thriving Rug Hookers Guild in Ontario, Canada.

In the 1970s two American textile historians claimed hooked rugs to be 'America's one indigenous craft';

one of the arguments they put forward to substantiate this claim was that most English rug-makers were influenced by the commercial patterns that were being manufactured in the United States by the 1880s. These were stamped on to hessian and sold in the same way as tapestry kits are nowadays. The patterns were advertised in American magazines and in mail order catalogues. However, considering the fact that rag rug-making in Britain (not England, as stated by the American historians) was almost exclusively carried out by poorly paid industrial or agricultural workers, it seems most improbable that they ever saw the catalogues, let alone had enough money to actually purchase the patterns.

Contemporary textile artists are not content just to use conventional materials such as rags and yarn, but are also exploring the potential of working with plastic bags, rubber gloves, foil and other non-traditional materials. Such projects are adding a new dimension to the creative possibilities of using recycled materials. As well as the familiar hooking and prodding techniques, locker-needle and shuttle hooks are also being used more widely, and plaiting/braiding is another method of rug-making that is again popular.

In the North of England rag rug-making is being used to foster a sense of community spirit with rugs being made by groups of women who had no previous knowledge of the craft. Many of the rugs depict local scenes and events; others express the makers' feelings about themselves and their role in society in traditional or abstract ways. Schoolteachers have found that young children are especially attracted by the tactile quality of the craft.

More and more people are becoming aware of the exciting possibilities this environmentally friendly craft offers. I hope this book will encourage you to recycle your discarded clothes, dressmaking remnants and jumble or rummage sale 'bargains' into a rug or wallhanging as this will give you hours of pleasure both in the making and using. Don't just think in terms of rugs and wallhangings, however: as you will see, the techniques can be applied to many other household items such as cushions and even clothing and jewellery. Rag rug-making is a craft in which both traditional and non-traditional materials can be used, and one with unlimited opportunities for experimentation and self-expression.

MATERIALS AND EQUIPMENT

THE BASIC materials and equipment required for making rag rugs or wallhangings are relatively inexpensive. The frame and hook are probably the most costly items, but they do not wear out, so you will not need to replace them. Obviously, if you do not have a rotary cutter and mat, a pair of scissors will suffice. If you become increasingly fascinated by this craft, you can add to your aids, possibly acquiring some of the more expensive items which are available in the US but not the UK, such as a gadget which cuts several strips of material at the same time, or a frame which sits comfortably on your lap.

MATERIAL

Rag rug-making is a thrift craft, which provides an ideal opportunity to use up any materials you have available, such as remnants left over from dressmaking, rummage sale bargains, or old blankets.

You will see by looking at the projects and the items illustrated in the Gallery that a wide selection of materials can be used in rag rug-making. Mostly woollens, jersey, felted jumpers and cardigans, worsteds, synthetics and blankets are used for rugs, but for other items such as wallhangings, cushions or jewellery, the fabric world is at your disposal. Cotton has been used in one or two of the projects but it is not advised for hooked or prodded work as it flattens and picks up the dirt easily. However, when used thickly as in the Garden Wallhanging project (see page 37), it has a charm of its own.

Woollen material is a wonderful medium in which to work when making rugs, but it is becoming an expensive commodity. Pure wool blankets were once often used but, since the introduction of continental quilts and duvets, they are getting scarcer. Scrap materials such as felted sweaters and other discarded clothes are also used – these should always be washed before using them for making rugs. Synthetics are often used nowadays but they have a much springier feel than wool.

If you are making a rug, you obviously need to use hard-wearing materials of similar thickness to keep the

. . . .

The joy of this craft is the range of materials that can be used, such as woollens, jersey, stretch fabrics, cotton, knitting wool, speciality yarns, panne velvet, leather, lurex, silks, netting and many more. Naturally the more exotic materials are not so appropriate for rugs but they may be incorporated into wallhangings, cushions and jewellery.

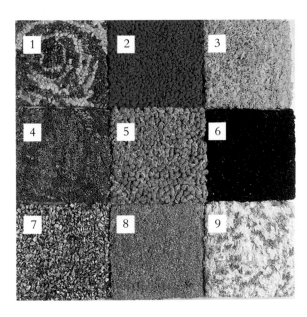

Traditionally hooked but not traditional materials, these small sample squares show what effects a little ingenuity can achieve.

1 *Computer print-out acetate: hooked but not cut*

2 *Shot nylon lining: hooked but not cut*

3 *Child's plastic raincoat: hooked and then loops cut*

4 *Rubber gloves: hooked and then loops cut*

5 *Denim jeans: hooked but not cut*

6 *Plastic bin liners: hooked and then loops cut*

7 *Crisp/chip and sweet/candy wrappers: hooked but not cut*

8 *Dishrags: hooked and then loops cut*

9 *Plastic bags: hooked and then loops cut*

. . . .

pile fairly level, but if you are making a wallhanging, you can use whatever you wish to achieve the intended effect. Lurex, netting, organza, sweet/candy wrappers, leather, metallic foil, raffia, crisp/chip packets, polythene and Lycra have all been used by rag rug-makers. The possibilities are indeed endless and it is often a matter of experimenting to see what can be used. If wondering whether a material is suitable, just 'hook it and see'!

If using discarded clothing, first remove all the buttons and other fastenings, and unpick the seams. Always wash any material that has been used. (Before putting old blankets in a washing machine, make sure that the edges are not frayed as loose fibres could clog up the machine.)

FRAMES

Three types of frame can be used, all of which are illustrated in the different projects in this book. Frames should always be larger than the dimensions of your rug to allow for hems and turnings.

The cheapest and easiest frame is formed from four artist's stretchers, which are available from any good art and craft supplier. They are already mitred and just have to be fitted together. You must remember, however, that you have to be able to reach into the centre of the frame when hooking rugs. You can make a rug as long as you like but the width is limited to the length of your arm. Creating a particularly large rug can be a problem unless you have a special large frame. One solution is to work one area, and then remove the hessian/burlap from the frame and reposition the unworked area of hessian over the frame, repeating the process as necessary to complete the rug. Or, you could work your rug in sections and sew them together afterwards. This does mean that there would be a weak spot where the material has been joined together. However, if you leave an unworked border all around a completed section, then lay the border of a second completed section on top of the first and hook through these two layers, this weakness will be avoided. (A word of warning though: hooking through two layers of hessian is not easy.)

Another type of frame is comprised of four pieces of wood, two with holes punched at varying intervals and two made of heavier wood with channels for the hessian and dowelling. These frames are available in various sizes. They are very useful because of the ease of putting in the hessian and the fact that the material can be rolled over one end so that rugs of varying lengths can be made.

The third type of frame is similar to the above but has strong braid attached to the two short ends, like an embroidery slate frame. The hessian is sewn on to the braid on two sides, then the two stretcher bars are attached on the remaining sides.

It is not advisable to use an embroidery hoop, except when working small pieces such as jewellery, as in the project on page 33.

MASKING TAPE

TRACING PAPER

GRAPH PAPER

PEN

METAL-EDGE
RULER

STAPLE GUN

STAPLES

DRAWING PINS

STAPLE REMOVER

HOOK

FELT-
TIP
MARKER

TRANSFER
PENCIL

RUG NEEDLE

PRODDER

LATCH
HOOK

LOCKER-
NEEDLE
HOOK

WALL
(CUP)
HOOK

ROTARY
CUTTER

SCISSORS

SHEARS

ARTIST'S STRETCHERS

22

LATEX/PVA GLUE   CUTTING MAT

STRING

HESSIAN/BURLAP

CARPET
BINDING

THREAD

SHUTTLE
HOOK

WOODEN KNITTING NEEDLE

TAPESTRY
CANVAS

DRESSMAKER'S
PINS

THIMBLE

GREY
POLYESTER
BACKING

KILT PIN

TAPE-MEASURE

CARD

LOOM

COMPASS

SPECIALIST FRAME

BASE AND BACKING MATERIAL

The material used most frequently is hessian (known as burlap in the United States, and brin in Newfoundland). Always buy the best quality you can obtain; do not be tempted to use cheap upholstery hessian. For hooking and prodding, any even-weave material can be used providing the mesh is not too tight. If you want to fill in a design but not its background, in a particular project, furnishing fabrics are worth considering as a base.

Grey polyester is sometimes used for hooking and was used for the project on page 73. It is slightly more expensive than hessian but some people are opposed to the latter on the grounds that it is possibly not as long-lasting as other materials – nonetheless, a hessian base will last many years.

Rug and tapestry canvas are used in some of the projects. Sacking can also be used, but again do not be tempted to use low-grade sacks. All sacking should be washed before use.

Backing fabrics can be used, though they are not crucial – carpet binding around the edges is usually sufficient. However, backing fabrics can be latexed on to the back of a completed piece to tidy and secure it if desired. Choose a material appropriate to the use – often hessian is used, or a polyester. A dual argument applies to the use of backing fabric: some say that by backing your rugs, grit can build up and act as an abrasive; others feel that it makes the rug longer-wearing.

HOOKS

The implement used for hooked rugs is similar to a crochet hook but has a much sharper point, like a barb. The ones illustrated in this book are handmade from yew and brass and fit nicely into your hand. Occasionally old hooks can be found in junk shops.

PRODDERS

The prodders illustrated are similar to the hook but without the barb. A sharply pointed piece of wood was often used as a prodder; this can be whittled from thick dowelling.

LATCH HOOK

The latch hook is the hook many people associate with rug-making, but not necessarily with rag rugs. As the latch hook has a deeper hook than the traditional one used for hooked rugs, it enables much wider pieces of cotton to be pulled easily through the rug canvas (it is not appropriate for use with hessian/burlap). A much bulkier effect is therefore achieved with this technique.

SHUTTLE HOOK

A shuttle hook is a simple articulated wood and metal tool which is used to make a series of loops through a hessian/burlap background. It is considered quicker than using the traditional hook. Little is known about the origin of this implement, but it was popular in the early part of this century, and in recent years there has been a revival of interest in this type of rug hooking. More difficult to obtain, shuttle hooks can be found in specialist suppliers.

. . . .

A shuttle hook in action: the design is worked from the reverse side of the base material. The shuttle is threaded with a strip of material, then operated by pushing first one section then the other into the base. The action is repeated with a 'walking' motion to produce a series of loops on the right side of the base material.

LOCKER-NEEDLE HOOK

The locker-needle hook is a relative newcomer to rag rug-making, having come on to the scene in the 1920s. Similar to a crochet hook at one end and large-eyed darning needle at the other, it makes a series of loops by pulling up fabric on to the hook which are then 'locked' by pulling yarn through the loops with the needle, thus preventing the loops falling back through the base material. This method gives a more woven appearance than the traditional hooked rug. Locker-needle hooks come in two sizes, one for finer work and one for rug-making.

CARPET BINDING

Often used for finishing off the edges of rugs, carpet binding can be obtained commercially or made at home. The binding should blend in with the colours used in your rug. If you cannot obtain the colour you require, then you can always dye the binding. Always wash commercial binding, remembering to purchase more than you require to go around the edge of your rug as it shrinks by up to 7.5cm (3in) per metre (yard) when washed.

If you want to make the binding yourself, use a strong material, always cut it on the bias and ensure that it is wide enough to allow for hemming on both sides and a generous overlap.

DYES

You can dye or overdye any material if liked, either by using a proprietary household brand or a more expensive professional dye. Dyeing for rag rug-making is generally not carried out as extensively in the UK as in North America. Some people use natural dyes but the process is time-consuming and not convenient for everyone.

LATEX/PVA GLUE

Latex can be used to seal the back of the rug. Polyvinyl acetate (PVA) woodworking glue, also known as white glue, can be used for the same purpose. One school of thought maintains that it is better not to use it because we do not know the long-term effects it will have on rugs; the other says that latex holds the loops in well and gives a longer-wearing surface. Some of the makers of these projects have used latex; others have not.

ROTARY CUTTER AND MAT

Available from patchwork suppliers, a rotary cutter and mat are a considerable help in cutting up material.

Rotary cutters are made in two sizes and it is advisable to use the larger size for cutting any material thicker than cotton. The rotary mat is self-sealing and is a necessary adjunct to the cutter. Again the mat is produced in two sizes, with marked divisions to act as guidelines for cutting material straight. The larger size is more useful.

SCISSORS AND SHEARS

A sharp pair of scissors is essential for cutting out material and snipping off ends. Some shears can also act as scissors.

TRANSFER PENCILS

These resemble old-fashioned transfers and are used to draw a design on tracing paper which is then transferred to the base fabric by pressing the design transfer-side down with a hot iron.

STAPLE GUN, STAPLES OR DRAWING PINS

Some people find a staple gun and staples very useful when fixing backing material to artist's stretchers, but others either do not want to go to the expense or find they are a little hard to use. Drawing pins can be used instead. Make sure that you place the staples or pins very close to each other and pay particular attention to the corners.

If you have used staples, you will find a staple remover a great help; an old screwdriver is useful for removing drawing pins.

MISCELLANEOUS

For some projects a sewing machine is useful. An iron is used for pressing (for which you need a pressing cloth). Other necessary items of equipment are needles, including a large-eyed carpet needle; strong thread for sewing on bindings and hemming; string; a compass for drawing circles; wooden knitting needle; tape-measure; dressmaker's pins; sticky and cotton tape; drawing, graph and tracing papers; thimble; thin and medium card; waterproof felt-tip pens (for outlining the dimensions of your rug or wallhanging, drawing round templates, and touching up any faint lines when using a transfer pencil or marking out centres). In one project white chalk is used for marking out a design.

BASIC TECHNIQUES

THE TWO main rag rug-making techniques – hooking and prodding – are described in this section, together with details of how to stretch your base material on different types of frame. Advice is also given on choosing colours, materials and designs. Step-by-step instructions on the less common rug-making techniques are given in the projects.

CHOOSING COLOURS

Colour and texture are of great importance in this craft. The texture of a particular material can often spark off an idea for a design, and the effect of a fabric can be transformed when hooked or prodded: a piece of tweed, for instance, when hooked, can look like the scales of a trout. The width of the strips of material can sometimes change the character of your work, too. It is very much a matter of developing an eye for colour and texture. It is advisable to keep a scrapbook of any magazine illustrations, postcards, or photographs that appeal to you, to remind you of ideas for using colour or of designs that could be adapted to a rug, wallhanging or other article. Any sample pieces of hooking should also be kept for reference.

To use colour effectively in your work means you should allow either warm or cool colours to predominate. Warm colours are those which are generally considered to be bold – reds, oranges and yellows. Cool colours are the various shades of blue, purple and green which are submissive and retreat into the background. Nowadays colour rules are often broken; this can result either in very vibrant pieces of work or, if you are not careful, the overall effect can appear discordant and harsh.

Once you have decided on a colour scheme, plan how to distribute the colours. Use colours with caution, looking at how they relate and react to each other. Your colour scheme may not only be dictated by your available materials, but also by where the rug will be placed. (If it is to be put in a much-used area, you may not want to use light-coloured materials.) A good method of trying out colours is to spread small pieces of the material you are considering using on the floor of the room in which the rug will be placed. Arrange the colours in a way in which you think they look best together, then stand back and consider the composition. You will easily see any colours that are either too bright or too dull. Add or subtract colours until you obtain a pleasing combination.

MAKING STRIPS

As a general rule, the material should be cut on the straight, not on the bias. The exceptions are mentioned in the relevant projects. Always ensure that you have enough of your chosen material. It is difficult to estimate the quantity you will need as this depends on so many factors such as the height of the loops and the type of material, but a useful rule of thumb is to fold your chosen material in four and place it on your background base material – this will give an approximation of the area it will cover.

Whatever material you are using, experiment before you cut all the fabric. With some synthetic jerseys you will have to cut wider strips to compensate for their stretching qualities. A useful general width is 5mm (¼in), but if you are using a thicker material, you may have to experiment to find the best width. Fraying materials have to be cut slightly wider; they should be turned under to give an edge for the hook to bring up to the front. Some people like to work with narrow strips, others with wider ones. It is very much a personal choice. Where possible, tear the material to get a straight edge; however, this is not possible with synthetics or jerseys. The length of strips can vary – generally it is best if they are over 15cm (6in), but they can be as long as you wish.

Before you tack the backing material down, it is a good idea to store a few strips of the material used in the hooking between the rug and the backing. Then, if you have any disasters in the future and your rug gets marked or damaged in any way, you have some strips of matching material for running repairs.

DYEING

If you do not care for the colour of any material, you can dye or overdye it. Of course if, for instance, you are using yellow dye on a blue material, the result will be not yellow but a shade of green. White or cream material is ideal for dyeing.

You can also try removing the colour from material by putting it in a large pan of water to which a few tablespoons of ammonia are added, and allowing the material to simmer (not boil) for a couple of minutes. You will be surprised by how much colour comes out. Rinse the material well and then set the new colour by simmering for about half an hour in a vinegar or salt bath. You only need to add a couple of tablespoonsfuls of either to the water, which should cover the fabric. (Salt turns the colour slightly grey, while vinegar brightens it.) Rinse well. This method works better with natural or mixed fibres than with synthetics. If the colour is very difficult to move, use a commercial dye remover.

DESIGN CONSIDERATIONS

A simple design can look just as impressive as a more complicated one. Obviously, when planning a rug or wallhanging, you have to bear in mind where you intend to place the finished article. Is the rug going to be seen from all angles or only from one position? Do you want it to be rectangular, oval, circular or another shape? (You will generally find that a square is not a pleasing shape for a rug.) You should also decide whether, in the case of rugs, you want a border and if so, of what width. A border should not dominate the rest of the rug but equally it should not be so narrow that it looks lost.

There are many aids to designing, including patchwork templates, French curves, cut paper shapes, ordinary household articles such as cups and saucers,

The fun of using discarded clothing or off-cuts of material is experimenting with dyes. Here some pieces of bright orange material have been simmered in a proprietary brand of dye remover, and taken out of the pan at various intervals to produce a range of shades which all blend with each other.

compasses and even fallen leaves. Since the advent of photocopiers with enlargement features, a small design – even a doodle – can be enlarged to act as a basis for design. Avoid anything too fussy, and keep your background simple if the other elements are 'busy'. Do your preliminary sketch in pencil and then, when you are satisfied, use a waterproof felt-tip pen to go over the design. With prodded rugs, remember that, because they have a shaggy pile, the design needs to be much simpler and will have less delineation. Often a pleasing result can be achieved just by using colour skilfully, although simple shapes, animals and flowers can be very effective, too.

PUTTING BASE MATERIAL ON A FRAME

In any project in which a frame is used, the base material must be stretched very tautly, to facilitate the entry of the hook or other implement. If using artist's stretchers for the frame, the base material should be the same size as the outside edge of the frame to ensure that the weft and warp of your material are straight. Using the edge of the frame as a guide, staple or pin the hessian/burlap on to it, working first down one width and one length. Then, pulling the hessian very taut, pin or staple the other two sides.

Place your frame in a good light in front of you. Make sure you are sitting comfortably, not hunched over the frame. You may find that leaning the frame against the edge of a table or over the two arms of an armchair is helpful.

. . . .

It is essential to ensure the edges of the hessian/burlap are straight when placed on a frame, otherwise the base material will become distorted as you work.

To ensure a straight edge, ease a thread from one side of the hessian gently and pull it out. When you have pulled the thread out, you will see this leaves a line which can be used as an accurate cutting guide.

. . . .

TRANSFERRING THE DESIGN

If you are not confident about outlining a design freehand, there are several ways to transfer a design on to the base fabric. Templates of shapes can be simply cut out in stiff card, placed on the backing and drawn around with a waterproof felt-tip pen. Or, a transfer pencil (which will transfer the design on to the fabric when a hot iron is used, rather like old-fashioned transfers) can be used to draw around the design on tracing paper or greaseproof paper. Pin the paper carefully to the backing with the transfer-side down, and go over the design with a hot iron. Check it is being transferred by lifting up a corner to see if the transfer appears on the hessian/burlap. If, when completed, the lines are a little faint, draw around them with a waterproof felt-tip pen.

HOOKING TECHNIQUE

1 Hold a strip of material in one hand loosely between your forefinger and thumb, under the hessian/burlap where your hook will enter. Holding the hook in the other hand as you would a pencil, and working from the front side, push the hook firmly through the hessian. Do not be too gentle: it is essential that you make a nice big hole. If you do not, the barb could catch on the threads when you pull the hook back up. Find the strip of material with the hook and bring one end of the material about 2.5cm (1in) through the hole up to the front.

2 Still holding the same strip of material loosely under the hessian, and working from right to left, leave two threads of the base mesh and then push your hook firmly into the hessian again. Catch the strip with the hook and pull it up tautly through the new hole to form a loop. Remove the hook from the loop. Repeat Steps 1 and 2.

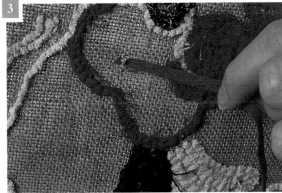

3 The reverse of the work shows how the hook completely catches the material to bring it up to the front. Don't attempt to feed the material on to the hook; instead, allow the hook to find the strip of material. The reverse of your work should look like rows of running stitches. If you have any loops appearing on the reverse, this means you are not pulling your material up firmly enough to the front of the work. If you find you are pulling out your previous loops, this means you are holding the strip of material tightly instead of allowing it to run loosely between your thumb and forefinger.

4 Continue working from right to left until you reach the end of the material strip. Bring the end of the material up to the front. To begin a new strip, push the hook into the same hole as the end of the previous strip and bring the new strip end up alongside it. Continue hooking as before. 'In, scoop, loop' will help you to remember the whole movement.

5 Cut any single ends that are showing so that they are level with the loops.

6 Leave about two threads between each row of hooking. If using wider strips of material, you should leave a few more threads between the loops and rows. Remember the loops must be close enough together so that you do not see the base material, but not so closely packed that they make the material 'hump'.

Never be tempted to carry strips of material across the back of the base material from one point to another; you could push your hook into them and accidentally pull out a lot of loops.

PRODDING TECHNIQUE

1 Working from the reverse side, and holding the prodder as you would a pen, push it firmly into the hessian/burlap, making a nice large hole.

2 Using the prodder, push one end of a cut strip of material firmly into the hole you have made, from the reverse to the front.

3 Using the fingers underneath the hessian, pull the strip halfway through – in other words to the right side of the work.

4 Leaving about two threads of the hessian mesh, and still working on the reverse of the work, push the prodder in again to make another large hole. Push the other end of the strip through to the right side and again pull it from underneath, so that it is level with the first end.

5 Push the prodder into the second hole with a new strip of material and repeat Steps 2, 3 and 4. (Two strips will therefore come through each hole.)

6 When repeated these steps make the shaggy pile which appears on the right side of the rug.

. . . .

How materials look when hooked

Around the outer edges of the photograph are the original materials and, adjacent to them, the same materials when hooked. It is always fascinating to see the effects achieved by hooking different materials. When in doubt about the suitability of any material, just work up a small piece to see the effect; keep these samples in a notebook for future reference.

GALLERY

THE PIECES of work illustrated on the following pages show how contemporary designers, some of whom are amateurs, use scraps of material and even discarded packaging to make rugs and wallhangings. These examples have been chosen to convey the diversity of artistic expression that can be achieved in this medium. Examples of hand-hooked rugs made earlier this century are also featured and they serve to illustrate how the homely craft of rag rug-making has developed into a recognized textile art form, offering virtually limitless opportunities for experimentation.

Once you have mastered the simple basic techniques, you will hopefully feel inspired to begin creating designs that reflect your own ideas.

~

Partridge in a Pear Tree
ANN DAVIES
79 × 56cm (31 × 22in)
This festive wallhanging was hooked with predominantly woollen fabrics, with details, for example the partridge's plummage, highlighted in lurex. Aran knitting wool was used to hook the light background.

GALLERY

Sun Ray

LIZZIE REAKES

50 × 50cm (20 × 20in)
Strong, vibrant colours
and the use of bold
symbols, such as arrows
and stars, in abstract
geometrical designs are
the hallmarks of Lizzie's
creations. She works
specifically with recycled
materials, and finds that
the incorporation of
materials such as plastics
and foil packaging
produces very durable
rugs. The materials are
also very tightly hooked
creating a dense, textured
finish.

. . . .

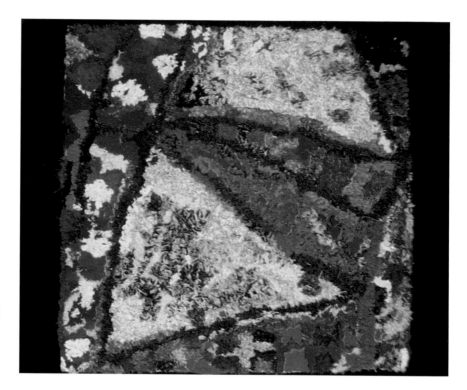

Big Apple

JOAN MOSHIMER

*65 × 108cm (25½ ×
42½in)*
Designed and made by
one of America's foremost
rug hookers, this unusual
semi-circular piece is very
finely hooked with
purpose-dyed materials
and finished with a tweed
border. The painterly
design features fruit,
flowers and insects.

. . . .

. . . .

La Mer

LYNNE STEIN

128 × 126cm (50½ × 49½in)

Hand-tufted and hooked using new and recycled materials and yarns, including silk, this richly textured and highly detailed figurative design could be mistaken, at first glance, for a piece of heavily worked embroidery.

. . . .

Greenstar

LIZZIE REAKES

About 74cm (29in) in diameter

The designer of this hand hooked wallhanging or rug finds star shapes a particular source of inspiration. Plastics and foils are included in the multi-coloured materials used to create the random patterns which fill the star points.

. . . .

. . . .

Angel With Six Stars

WINIFRED PRATT

76 × 56cm (30 × 22in)
Although quite simple in
outline and colouring, this
design is nevertheless
extremely striking and is
unusual in that it
incorporates lettering as a
border feature; hand-
hooked with wool and
synthetic materials.

. . . .

Baltimore Beauty

ANN DAVIES

104 × 107cm (41 × 42in)
Based on stylized floral
motifs taken from a North
American patchwork
design, this large rug was
hooked in the traditional
way. An old blanket was
dipped in weak tea to give
an antique linen look to
the creamy background.

. . . .

Stained Glass Flowers

ANN DAVIES

91cm (36in) in diameter

A book of stained glass designs provided the inspiration for this hooked circular wallhanging. Only woollen materials were used, with black wool simulating the lead used in windows.

. . . .

Mexicano Mat

LYNNE STEIN

About 119 × 114cm (47 × 45in)

Rags, fibres and metallic fabrics are incorporated in this hand-hooked rug, commissioned to enhance a range of interior designer wallcoverings by Timmey-Fowler. The vibrant clashing colours express the vitality of Latin America.

. . . .

Lava Flow

ANN DAVIES

79 × 56cm (31 × 22in)

In this traditionally hooked wallhanging the force of the lava flow is emphasized by the asymmetrical design executed in a wide range of materials of different weights such as heavy coating and organza.

. . . .

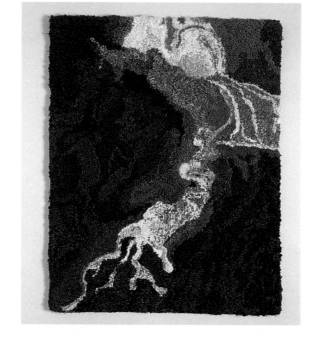

The Frith

CHRISTINE ELLIS

About 183 × 61cm (72 × 24in)

The window frame used in this locker-needle hooked picture creates the illusion that the muted colours of the autumnal landscape are seen through glass. Other subjects – for example, a seascape – could be treated in the same way equally successfully.

. . . .

Set-of-Three

UNKNOWN MAKER

150 × 94cm (59 × 37in);
91 × 86cm (36 × 34in);
91 × 43cm (36 × 17in)
Old examples of matching
rug sets are extremely
rare. These three rugs, of
varying sizes, all feature
the same stylized daisy
motif and colour
treatment. They are
thought to date to the
1930s, and were hand-
hooked using tweed and
other woollen materials.

. . . .

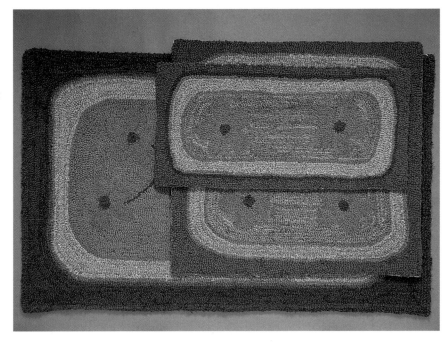

Mock Oriental

UNKNOWN MAKER

135 × 94cm (53 × 37in)
Made around 1910, a
simplified oriental carpet
design was probably the
inspiration for this hand-
hooked rug, which
incorporates a variety of
materials, including wool
and jersey.

. . . .

CUSHION COVER

ANN DAVIES

THIS DESIGN was adapted from a motif on a Chinese rug. By using strong colours it has been given a contemporary look but if you chose softer colours, the design would seem totally different and more oriental in appearance. The shape of the design could also be adapted easily for a round cushion. Alternatively, the motif used here could be repeated several times to make a rug. Tweeds, plaids and plain woollen materials were used in this cushion cover.

This may be a good hooked project with which to start, as a cushion cover obviously takes less time to make, and its straightforward design is more accessible than other more ambitious pieces of work.

46 × 46cm (18 × 18in)

~

MATERIALS AND EQUIPMENT

- *floral design* • *tracing paper*
- *transfer pencil* • *61 ×*
61cm (24 × 24in) hessian/
burlap • *ruler* • *medium felt-*
tip pen • *iron* • *pins* • *staple*
gun and staples or drawing
pins • *4 × 61cm (24in)*
artist's stretchers • *rotary*
cutter, mat and metal-edge
ruler or scissors • *assortment*
of materials • *hook* • *49 ×*
49cm (19¼ × 19¼in)
backing material (to blend
with cushion colours)
- *sewing machine* • *needle*
- *matching cotton* • *thimble*
- *pressing cloth* • *46 × 46cm*
(18 × 18in) cushion pad

· · · · ·

1 Draw your design on to tracing paper, using a transfer pencil. Because this design is symmetrical, it is not necessary to reverse it.

Keeping the threads of the hessian straight, use a ruler and felt-tip pen to mark the corners for the size of cushion cover you want. Then drag your pen down from one corner mark to another by pulling it between two threads (or use a ruler). You can mark the centre either by measuring across the width and length and marking with a pen, or by folding the hessian in half, first one way then the other, and lightly creasing it with a hot iron.

Place the design, traced-side down, on the hessian, matching the centres, and pin down to prevent it from slipping. Go over the design with a hot iron, lifting a corner to check that the design is being transferred on to the hessian.

2 Staple or pin the hessian on to the assembled stretchers, leaving at least 10cm (4in) all around the finished design and keeping the threads as straight as possible (see page 87).

3 Cut your material into strips about 5mm (¼in) wide. You can either use a rotary cutter, mat and metal-edge ruler to cut several folds of material in one go, or cut single strips with scissors. Do not cut all your strips at once; you do not really know how much you will be using. Do, however, make sure you have enough material to finish the project.

4 Commence by hooking the outline (see page 17).

5 Continue to build up the design. If you work some of the detail and then some of the background, you will avoid being left with all the boring background to complete at once! When the design is finished, remove the hessian from the frame and cut the hessian down to about 4cm (1½in) all around the marked square.

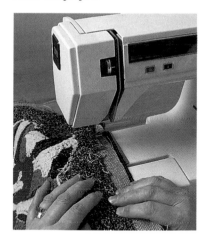

6 Place the right side of the backing material against the right side of the work, and pin or tack all around. Using a sewing machine (or you could sew by hand, using strong thread), stitch round three sides very close to the last row of hooking, securing the beginning and end with an overstitch.

7 Cut the hessian and backing material to about 1cm (½in) on the three sides, leaving about 2.5cm (1in) on the fourth side (which has not been sewn down). Snip enough hessian from the corners to ensure there is no 'bump' when you turn the cushion cover right-side out. Having done so, paying particular attention to the corners, place the cushion cover right-side down on a towel or padded surface, cover with a damp cloth and press with a hot iron. Insert the cushion pad and slip-stitch the remaining side, turning the hessian and backing under so that they are not visible.

RAZZLE DAZZLE

LIZZIE REAKES

TRADITIONAL HOOKING techniques are applied here on a small scale, to create innovative jewellery. Showing how a classic craft can be adapted and updated to devise something truly contemporary, the artist has used waste packaging material. Instead of recycled rags and wool, these environmentally friendly pieces are made from sweet and candy wrappers, wrapping paper, foil and plastic shopping bags.

~

MATERIALS AND EQUIPMENT

● pencil ● thin card ● scissors ● assortment of wrapping papers, packaging and shiny materials ● 3 small pieces of hessian/burlap, each slightly larger than the hoop ● 25cm (10in) embroidery hoop ● cotton tape ● thick felt-tip pen ● hook ● latex/ PVA glue ● 3 small pieces of velvet, slightly larger than the designs ● quick-drying glue ● jewellery findings (pins or ear-clips)

. . . . . .

1 Draw out your jewellery shapes on thin card to the sizes required, and cut out as templates. Simple shapes are best.

2 Cut your materials into strips, about 1cm (½in) wide.

3 Place a piece of hessian in the embroidery hoop. It is advisable to wind cotton tape around the inner hoop to stop the hessian from slipping. Tighten the hoop as much as you can. Place a template in the centre – here the heart-shaped brooch – and draw around it with a felt-tip pen. Start hooking (see page 17) from the centre outwards.

4 The back of the work (as shown here) may look a little more loopy than in traditional hooking; this is due to the stiffness of the materials being used. However, try to make the back as neat as you can.

5 Continue to build up your design, juxtaposing colours and materials in a balanced way.

6 Remove the completed piece from the hoop and cut around the shape, leaving a narrow hem. Turn the hem under – you may have to snip it in places to ease it – and cover the back with a layer of latex. Place latex-side down on to the back of a piece of velvet.

7 Holding the hooked piece and the velvet together, cut around the shape very close to the edge, trying to cut at an angle so that no velvet shows on the front. Then, using a quick-drying glue, attach the chosen brooch finding to the back and leave to dry.

The same method is used for both the earrings and hair slide shown in the photograph on page 32. You can of course work a pair of earrings on the same piece of hessian.

GARDEN WALLHANGING

ANITA FELL

THE LATCH hook (see page 12) is used to create this spectacular piece of work, though the hook is not used in the conventional manner, as the latch is actually taped out of the way. (Because fabric is being used rather than yarn, the pressure of the bunched-up material in the hole will keep the loops in place without the need for knot-tying with the latch hook.) The flowers and foliage areas are clipped to make a contrast to the worked loops. Cotton is mainly used but other materials are also included.

This particular piece is being used as a rug, but it would also make a marvellous wallhanging. The design can be adapted to suit other subjects such as an open doorway. This rug is life-size, but you can scale it down and omit a few rows of brickwork or reduce the area of foliage if you require something smaller.

142 × 107cm (56 × 42in)

~

MATERIALS AND EQUIPMENT

- *pencil* • *drawing paper*
- *150 × 115cm (59 ×*
45¼in) rug canvas, gauge 3
holes to 2.5cm (1in) • *thick*
felt-tip pen • *latch hook*
- *sticky tape* • *assortment of*
rags and fabric remnants in
shades required • *scissors*
- *150 × 115cm (59 ×*
45¼in) backing fabric • *pins*
- *needle* • *strong sewing*
thread • *For wallhanging*
(optional): 100cm × 15cm
(39½ × 6in) calico or
similarly strong fabric;
wooden dowel or flat wooden
bar, 105cm (41½in) long;
2 large closed-ring picture-
hanging screws; 210cm
(82¾in) strong cord

. . . . . .

1 Sketch out your design on paper as a guide, and then, using a thick felt-tip pen, draw the outlines of the bricks on the canvas. The mesh will help you to make the lines straight. You can then mark in the flowers and the edge of the foliage.

2 On both the shorter sides (top and bottom) of the design, turn under a 4–hole-wide strip, making sure that the holes line up exactly on both layers of the canvas mesh. (You will hook your strips through this double layer.) On both the longer sides, leave a 4-hole-wide strip between the edge of your rug canvas and your design. If you want to create a wallhanging, however, turn under the long sides as described and leave the shorter ones open.

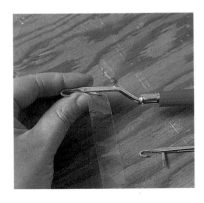

4 Cut or tear the fabric into strips. These can be any length but the width should vary according to the weight of the fabric. For example, lightweight material such as nylon should be cut in wider strips than thick woollen cloth. It is advisable to cut a short strip of every fabric first to check whether the width is correct. If it is too wide, it will distort the canvas mesh, and if too narrow, it will not stay in place securely and the canvas mesh background will be visible.

3 Wrap the latch on your hook out of the way with sticky tape. This part of the hook is not used in this project.

5 Hold a strip of fabric in one hand under the canvas mesh at the back – you work with the front facing you – and with the other hand insert the hook down through one hole. (The advantage of using rug canvas is that you can see through it!). Catch the end of the strip and pull it through to the front, to a height of about 1cm (½in). Insert the hook into the next hole and catch up the strip of the fabric, ensuring that the whole width of the fabric is on the hook.

6 Pull the loop through, to a minimum height of 1cm (½in). Then insert your hook into the next hole and catch the strip further along its length. Pull through and repeat, making sure all your loops are a similar size. Hook all the raw ends of the strips through to the front and cut them off evenly, so that they align with the loops, or with the surface of the pile.

7 Work along in rows, in any direction, in a random mixture of terracotta, red and brown shades to build up the bricks, and in cream for the lines of mortar.

8 Check the back of your work regularly to make sure that the whole width of the strip has been pulled through to the surface of the pile. The underside should show flat loops pulled taut against the canvas.

9 To make the plants stand out in three-dimensional relief from the wall and to add a contrast of texture, hook the foliage and flower loops slightly higher than the brickwork and shear off the top surface horizontally to make clipped tufts. If you prefer, you can insert your scissors into each loop and cut them individually. It is possible to sculpt the surface like topiary to create a variety of heights and textures.

10 When complete, turn the unworked edges on two sides under the back of the rug, using your fingers to press them down firmly.

11 Place the rug upside down on the floor and lay the backing fabric on top, making sure the grain of the fabric lies square to the canvas mesh. Working outwards from the centre of one of the sides worked right to the edge, pin the backing to the edge of the rug, turning under a hem of 4cm (1½in) as you go. When you reach the corner, then work from the centre of the side at right angles to it, turning under and pinning the unworked 4-hole border of canvas mesh. Finish the other sides in the same way. Do not make the backing too taut as this would cause the edges of the rug to curl inwards, but check that the fabric is flat with no puckering. Slip-stitch the edge of the backing to the edge of the rug with strong thread.

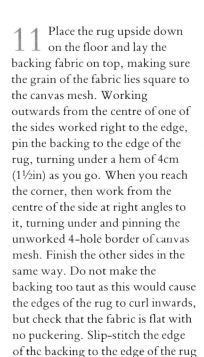

12 If you are going to display your rug as a wallhanging (see Step 2), it is advisable to attach a fabric sleeve to the back. When complete, cut a piece of strong fabric such as calico, and hem the raw edges. Place this 7cm (2¾in) from and parallel with the top edge of the rug. Slip-stitch this along both long sides, leaving the short edges open. As you sew, occasionally take the thread through the backing and secure it to the rug canvas for extra strength. A piece of wooden dowelling can then be inserted through the sleeve so that it protrudes equally at each end. Attach a closed-ring picture screw at each end and thread strong cord through these, keeping it fairly taut so that the method of hanging will be invisible from the front.

'BROKEN GLASS' RUG

ANN DAVIES

ODDS AND ENDS of woollen material left over from other projects were used to make this traditional-type hooked rug. However, it is worked with much narrower strips of material than is usually found in old hooked rugs. By hooking the outlines in black or another dark colour, rather than beige, the design could be made to look bolder.

No traced design is really necessary for this rug; you just have to outline the dimensions of the rug and then break up the surface into pleasing shapes, using a felt-tip pen. Outline all the shapes in the same colour and then fill them in with whatever materials you have available. This idea could also be adapted for cushion covers, chair seats or possibly even a tea cosy!

98 × 80cm (38½ × 31½in)

~

MATERIALS AND EQUIPMENT

- *106 × 91.5cm (42 × 36in) hessian/burlap* • *medium black felt-tip pen* • *tape-measure* • *medium-sized frame* • *assortment of materials* • *scissors or rotary cutter and mat* • *hook* • *4.5 metres (5 yds) carpet binding tape* • *strong linen thread* • *darning needle* • *thimble* • *iron* • *towel or blanket* • *pressing cloth*

. . . . . .

1 As the design used for this rug does not require a pattern to be traced, just outline the required dimensions directly on to the hessian. Allow about 10cm (4in) extra all around when you have marked the actual size. Then sketch in the 'broken glass' design in a variety of pleasing shapes.

2 Fit the hessian into the frame, rolling the surplus material around one end and stretching the fabric. Cut your chosen outlining material on the straight into strips about 5mm (¼in) wide, and begin to hook in the outlines (see page 17).

3 Cut up the materials you intend to use for filling in the shapes. You may have some strips left over from other projects and this design is a wonderful way of using them up. Aim for a pleasing mixture of colours, and avoid putting all–light or all–dark strips adjacent to each other. Begin to hook in the inside areas of colour.

Pull up your loops to a height that appeals to you – not too high so that people could catch their heels in the pile and not so low that the pile will wear quickly. A height of about 5mm (¼in) is usual.

4 The reverse of your work (shown here) should look like running stitches. If any loops are showing on the back, then you are not pulling these up sufficiently to the front of the rug. Always bring the ends of the strips up to the front of the work.

5 Continue to fill in the spaces. When you have completed the part of the rug that is visible in the frame, take out the side pieces of the frame and roll the finished part over the opposite side of the frame to the one on which the spare hessian is rolled. Re-frame and begin again.

6 When you have completed all the hooking, remove the rug from the frame. Your carpet binding should be a colour that blends in with your design and should have been washed previously to allow for the shrinkage; you lose about 7.5cm (3in) to the metre (yard). Using a strong thread and a hem stitch, sew the binding on the right side as close to the last row of hooking as you can. Do not begin to sew the binding at a corner, but start halfway along one edge.

7 Ease the binding around the corners of the rug; do not allow any excess for mitring.

8 Cut off the excess hessian to about 5cm (2in) all around, cutting across the corners to prevent a build-up of material there.

9 First turn down the hessian on to the back of the rug and tack it down, catching the hessian lightly to the reverse of the rug. Do not take the stitches through to the front. You will see in the photograph how the hessian has been cut away at the corners.

10 Then turn the binding down over the hessian and hem it down, again catching the stitches in the reverse of the rug. Coax the excess binding at each corner into a mitre and catch it down. You can then sew over the mitred corners, if liked. Hem the binding all around the rug ensuring the binding covers the turned down hessian.

11 Place the rug right-side down on a towel or blanket and, using a damp cloth, press all over with an iron.

STAR-BURST RUG

LIZZIE REAKES

THIS EXUBERANTLY modern hooked rug is worked in a traditional way but with a variety of different materials, many of them acrylics. After hooking, the rug is completely sheared and the back sealed. Shearing is quite tiring for the hands but the effort involved is worthwhile when a rug like this is produced.

So many rag rugs are rectangular that it is good to have a design for a different shape. This rug looks most effective on a light pine floor in a modern room.

107cm (42in) in diameter

~

MATERIALS AND EQUIPMENT

● *drawing paper* ● *coloured pencils* ● *thick felt-tip pen* ● *ruler* ● *ball of string* ● *scissors* ● *127 × 127cm (50 × 50in) hessian/burlap* ● *drawing pin* ● *thin card* ● *frame with dowelling* ● *dressmaker's pins* ● *sewing machine* ● *hook* ● *assortment of materials* ● *127 × 127cm (50 × 50in) hessian for backing* ● *latex/PVA glue*

. . . . . .

1 For this rug, sketch the design on drawing paper to size and colour it to act as a guide for hooking the materials. To create a rough circle shape, mark the centre of the design with a felt-tip pen, then measure the distance from the centre to the edge with string, allowing a little extra to make a loop to tie round the pen.

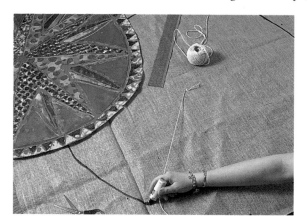

2 Cut the string and make a loose knot at the opposite end to the pen. Lay the hessian on a protected surface. Place a drawing pin in the knot of the string and press into the centre of the hessian. Tie the other end to the felt-tip pen and then draw a circle carefully as if using a compass.

3 Using the same technique, draw another circle about 15cm (6in) inside the previous one to mark the border. Trace and cut out the main shapes of the star-burst design in thin card, place them on the hessian and trace around them with a felt-tip pen.

4 This rug is worked on a frame which uses dowelling to secure two of its edges. To make a channel to run the dowelling through, turn down the hessian on two sides (top and bottom if the design is rectangular), pin and machine across. Assemble the frame.

5 Using scissors, cut up some of your materials into strips about 1cm (½in) wide, ensuring they are always on the straight, never on the bias. Commence hooking (see page 17) from the centre outwards.

6 Continue your hooking until a reasonable amount has been worked.

7 Shear the loops by cutting across them as if you were cutting a lawn. It is a good idea to alternate shearing and hooking as you go.

8 This shows the final loop being put in place!

9 Complete the shearing around the edge and brush away the trimmings.

10 Remove the rug from the frame and lay face-down on a table. Place the piece of backing material on top of the rug. Feeling the shape with your felt-tip pen, draw around the rug. Cut out the shape in the backing material, the same size as the finished rug.

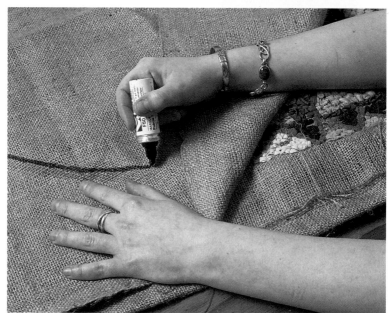

11 Remove the backing material and spread latex all over the reverse side of the rug. Make sure the surface is well covered but avoid using an excessive amount.

12 Lay the backing on to the latexed back and press it with a hot iron.

13 Cut the surplus hessian away from the worked rug, leaving about 15cm (6in) all around for turning. Snip the hessian at intervals all around the rug.

14 Apply latex to the cut edges and press them down firmly, slightly overlapping, as shown. Allow to dry.

LUCKY BLACK CAT

DEBBIE SINISKA

IN THIS project a shuttle hook (see page 12) makes the loops. The result looks like a traditional hooked work, but the technique is much quicker once you have mastered the knack of working with this type of hook. The frame must be leant against a wall or door as the shuttle hook has to pierce through the hessian/burlap or sacking freely. Long strips of fabric are used, working from the reverse, and the material is cut much wider than in other methods of rug-making.

All types of materials may be used in this project, but stretchy jersey fabrics or old jumpers are favoured by many users of the shuttle hook. The technique is mainly used for making rugs and wallhangings. A nice idea is to sprinkle dried lavender between the rug and its backing, for a lovely fragrance.

100 × 72cm (39½ × 28½in)

~

MATERIALS AND EQUIPMENT

- pencil ● drawing paper
- sacking (a peanut sack was used for this project) ● nail
- strong thread (if needed)
- large-eyed carpet needle
- frame ● strong string
- tracing paper ● piece of chalk ● assortment of stretchy materials ● shuttle hook
- latex/PVA glue ● sacking or hessian/burlap for lining, to the dimensions of the finished rug ● carpet binding

. . . . . .

1 Sketch out the design on drawing paper, as a guide.

2 Unpick the sacking with a nail or needle, if necessary, carefully removing any threads that hold it together.

3 Sew the sacking firmly to the binding on both ends of the frame using strong thread and a carpet needle. You can reuse the thread unpicked from the sacking, if wished.

4 Assemble the frame, stretching the sacking tautly between the two ends of the frame. Then, using strong string, lace the sacking firmly to the side bars.

5 You will need to reverse the design, as a shuttle hook works from the back of the base material. Trace the sketch on to tracing paper, then flip this over and press over the lines firmly on to a clean sheet of paper. Go over the impressed outline with a pencil to create a mirror-image. Then, transfer the reversed design to the sacking. If you are not confident about scaling-up freehand, draw a matching grid pattern on both the sketch and the sacking, then carefully copy the outline on to the larger background square-by-square with chalk.

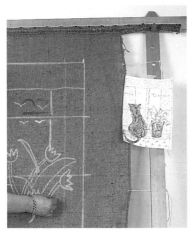

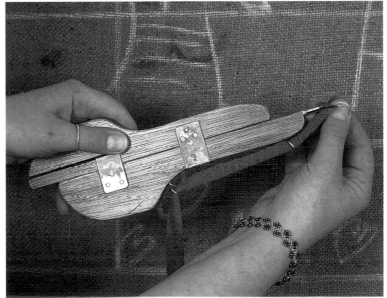

6 Cut your material on the straight into strips at least 1cm (½in) wide, and thread the shuttle hook as shown.

7 Set the frame so that it is leaning securely against a wall. Sit on a low stool, and holding your shuttle hook with both hands and leaving the end of the material free, slide one part of the shuttle hook into the sacking.

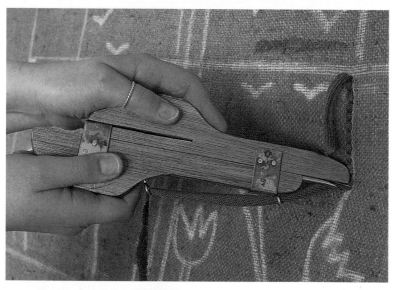

8 Without removing the shuttle hook, slide the second half of the shuttle hook into the sacking.

9 This double movement of the shuttle hook produces a loop on the front of the sacking, as shown here.

10 Continue making this double movement, 'walking' the shuttle hook across the sacking.

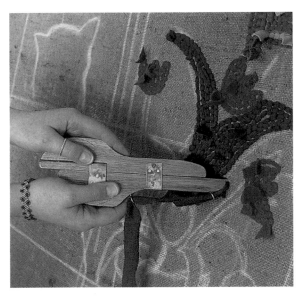

11 Because of the width of the strips of material it is not necessary to keep the rows as close together as you would with traditional hooking. You can work in any direction.

12 When the design is completed, remove the rug from the frame. Trim the hessian, allowing a 10cm (4in) border for turning.

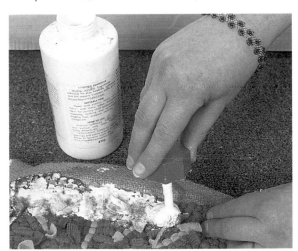

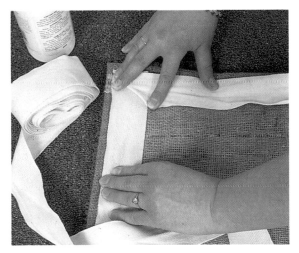

13 Lay the rug right-side down on the floor or a table. Apply latex generously to the edges of the rug back, turning the sacking down over it.

14 Now stick the backing fabric on to the reverse of the rug, using latex to secure it around the edges. To neaten the edges, stick carpet binding around the edges with latex, mitring the corners. Press down firmly.

EDGE OF THE RIVER

CHRISTINE ELLIS

THIS RUG is made by the unusual locker-needle hook technique (see page 12). Unlike most other rag rug methods, the base is a single (mono) tapestry canvas, 5 holes to 2.5cm (1in). The abstract design of this rug was inspired by a river-bank, with rushes and leaves against a blue and white background. Other themes and designs could be planned and developed using the same technique. Mainly cotton scraps have been used here, but many other materials are also appropriate. Locker hooking can be used for other articles as diverse as chair seats, cushions, handbags, wallhangings and articles of clothing.

136 × 76cm (53½ × 30in)

~

MATERIALS AND EQUIPMENT

● pencil ● drawing and graph paper ● 142.5 × 81cm (56 × 32in) rug canvas, 5 holes to 2.5cm (1in) ● thick waterproof felt-tip pen ● thin card or cartridge paper ● scissors ● masking tape ● double-knitting wool or rug yarn for the edges ● rug needle ● 2-ply rug yarn or equivalent ● locker-needle hook ● assortment of cotton and jersey materials ● 2 pieces lining material, 44cm (17¼in) wide (see Step 13)

. . . . . .

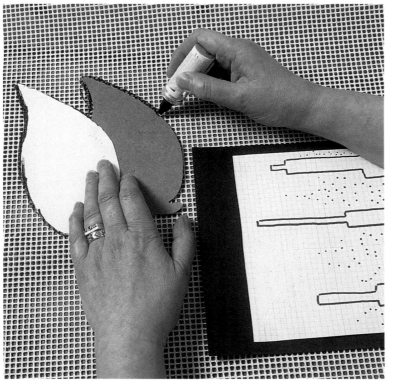

1 Draw a pencil sketch of your planned design for reference, then plot out the basic repeat structural outline on to graph paper. This graph outline can then be transferred to the canvas with a felt-tip pen; follow the design graph-square by mesh-square for an accurate result. Use real leaves as a guide to make paper or card templates, if wished, or draw them freehand and then cut out. You will need two templates for each leaf shape. (You will work from the front of the piece with this technique.)

2 Place the leaf-shaped templates on the canvas in the desired positions and draw around them with a waterproof felt-tip pen. Overlap the templates to prepare for the shadow effect shown on the completed canvas.

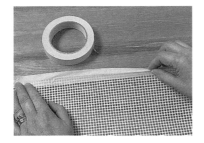

3 Before beginning work, you need to decide how to finish the edges. If you are not sure what size you want your finished rug to be, stick masking tape over the edges of the canvas to stop it unravelling and to prevent material from catching.

4 If, however, you are sure what size you want your rug to be, the edges can be secured now. Mitre all the corners of the hem, then using double-knitting wool or rug yarn and a rug needle, oversew three stitches over each corner. Then work an overlapping braid stitch all round. To do this, insert the needle from the back of the canvas to the front, move one hole to the left and bring the yarn back to the original hole. Then move three holes to the left, back two, and continue in this way, working over the stitches which are reinforcing the corners.

5 Thread two strands of 2-ply rug yarn through the eye of the locker-needle hook. Then, cut strips of material about 2cm (¾in) wide; straight or bias strips are equally successful. The finer the fabric, the wider the strip will have to be as the aim is to fill the holes and cover the canvas.

6 Holding a strip of cut material under the canvas in your left hand, dip the hook end of the locker-needle into a hole and catch and pull a small loop of material up through the canvas.

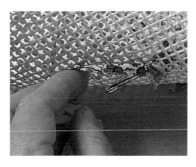

7 The reverse of the work shows how a hook is placed to pull up a loop of material. To ensure the loops are even and regular, keep the strip over the forefinger and pass it over the locker-needle hook, away from you.

8 Working from right to left, carry on making loops of material on the locker-needle hook and along the row, picking up a loop through each hole until there are ten or twelve loops on the hook. (In this design the leaves are worked in vertical and diagonal directions and the background is worked horizontally.)

9 At the end of a strip, gently pull the threaded locker-needle end through the loops, which will then be 'locked' in place with the yarn. Continue with a new row of loops, pulling up the loops on to the locker-needle hook and 'locking' them with the same length of yarn. Start new material strips as necessary, when another colour may be chosen.

10 Unlike traditional hooking, all the ends of the fabric material are left on the back with this technique, as shown here. When the hooking is completed, trim the ends to 2cm (¾in).

11 When either starting or finishing a new strand of yarn, leave the wool ends on the front of the rug. When several ends have accumulated, thread them through a blunt needle and run the yarn under four or so loops to secure them.

12 Then, clip off the remaining ends of yarn. As you proceed and the work becomes heavier, it is often more comfortable to have a small table in front of your chair, so that you can rest the bulk of the rug on the table and turn it to follow your usual working route from right to left.

13 Cut two pieces of lining fabric (closely woven cotton if the rug is to be used on a carpet; heavier material such as sailcloth, if on a concrete or tiled floor). The length of each piece should be half the length of the rug plus 7.5cm (3in), and the same width, with a further 2.5cm (1in) on all sides for the hem allowance. On each piece turn down and hem the end that will form the placket or central gap in the rug. Turn in the raw edges of the lining fabric and slip-stitch one piece to three sides of the rug, leaving the hemmed edge in the centre free. Repeat with the second piece, slightly overlapping at the centre. This gap means that both the inside and the surface of the rug can be cleaned with a vacuum.

BRIGHT AND BREEZY

JENNI STUART ANDERSON

IN THIS project, instead of hooking or prodding the material, the strips are plaited/braided before being sewn together to make a rug.

Cotton fabrics, from a blouse, dress, skirt and part of a duvet or continental quilt cover, were used to make a cheerful rug for a child's room. If you prefer to make a heavier rug, then you could use woollen or synthetic fabrics.

You could make similar plaited strips to form a border for a hooked or prodded rug.

66 × 52cm (26 × 20½in)

~

MATERIALS AND EQUIPMENT

• *scissors* • *assortment of cotton materials* • *tape-measure* • *needle* • *cotton thread* • *dressmaker's pins* • *large pin (safety, nappy or kilt)* • *wall (cup) hook* • *button thread* • *thimble*

. . . . . .

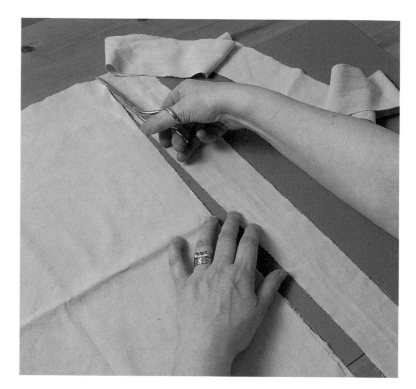

1 Cut the material into strips, 7cm (2¾in) wide. Sew the strips end-to-end to make lengths of about 2 metres (2¼ yds).

2 For each plait/braid, roll up three separate strips, leaving about 90cm (35½in) of the lengths unrolled. This will help to prevent the strips from becoming entangled while plaiting. Secure each roll with a pin.

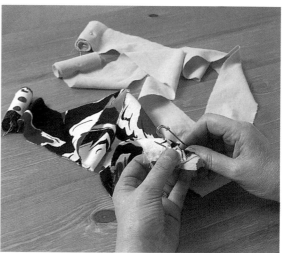

3 Using a large pin, fasten three of the strips together at the unrolled ends, ready to start plaiting.

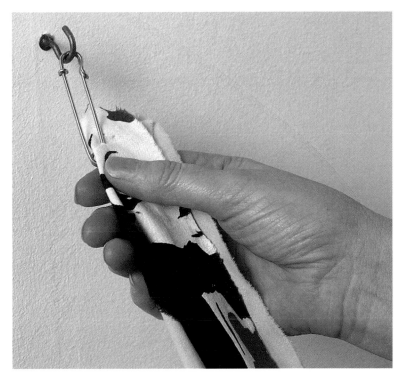

4 Hook the large pin over a wall or cup hook which you have screwed into a beam or door frame, just above eye level.

5 Turning the raw edges towards the back (away from you) as you work, start plaiting next to the large pin. This end of the plait will not be neat at this stage. First, bring the right strip over the middle strip.

6 Bring the left strip over the new middle strip and continue plaiting fairly loosely.

7 Remember to turn the raw edges back as much as you can, gradually unrolling the strips as you work. On reaching the ends of the strips, secure with a pin.

8 Arrange a selection of plaits on the table and move them around until you have a colour scheme that pleases you. Cut 16 plaits, each 53cm (21in) in length, securing the ends with pins so that they do not unravel. You must work with the plaits flat on a table, otherwise the rug will be mis-shapen. Using a needle and button thread, catch a little of one plait, then a little of the adjacent one, working from side to side and along the length to sew two plaits together. The stitches should not show. Repeat to secure all 16 plaits together.

9 Sew together the loose ends of all 16 plaits. Sew a 70cm (27½in) strip of fabric across the ends of the plaits at the top and bottom from the right side of the rug, using a simple back stitch.

10 Turn the fabric over to the back of the rug and hem down.

11 To prepare for the rug border, taper one end of a new long plait, and stitch it neatly.

12 Sew the long plait around the rug, using the same technique as in Step 8. Cut the plait a little beyond the point where the ends meet and taper one end neatly, sewing it to the other end of the plait. Sew two more plaits all around the rug, in the same way, staggering the places where the ends meet.

13 Place the rug face-down on the backing fabric and cut around the rug, leaving a border of 3cm (1¼in). Turn the rug over and pin the backing to the edge, turning it under and following the shape of the rug. Pin the backing to the rug at regular intervals. Using button thread, back-stitch lines about 6cm (2½in) apart across the rug at right angles to the plaits. This joins the plaits together more securely. Hem around the backing.

BLOSSOM TIME

ANN DAVIES

THIS PARTICULAR rug, featuring a contemporary technique, was inspired by a postcard showing spring blossom. Nearly every combination of colours is effective in this simple design. It is not, however, a quick technique and it uses up a great deal of material.

The choice of materials depends on how you want to use the finished article. For a rug, you would need an easy-to-clean material such as cotton, but if you wanted to adapt the idea for a wallhanging or cushion cover, it would be fun to experiment with different kinds of material such as lurex, netting, organza and other speciality fabrics. For the base fabric, choose grey polyester or any other even-weave material which is not too closely woven.

An American rug-maker, Gloria Crouse, created a similar technique but she sometimes outlines her circles with fabric paint which gives an added dimension. She also cuts some of her material into squares, and uses pinking shears to cut out some of the circles to give a different effect.

75 × 62cm (29½ × 24½in)

~

MATERIALS AND EQUIPMENT

● *stapler and staple gun or drawing pins* ● *87 × 71cm (34¼ × 28in) grey polyester* ● *2 × 86cm (34in) and 2 × 71cm (28in) artist's stretchers* ● *fine felt-tip pen* ● *compass* ● *soft pencil* ● *strong card* ● *scissors* ● *assortment of cotton material (have plenty)* ● *wooden knitting needle* ● *plastic knife* ● *latex/PVA glue* ● *piece of thin foam to size of finished rug* ● *79 × 66cm (31 × 26in) backing material (can be same material as rug)* ● *cotton thread* ● *needle* ● *thimble*

. . . . . .

1 Assemble the artist's stretchers and staple or pin the grey polyester to the frame, pulling it taut and keeping the threads straight (see page 87).

2 Draw the outline of the rug by running a felt-tip pen between two threads of grey polyester (or use a ruler).

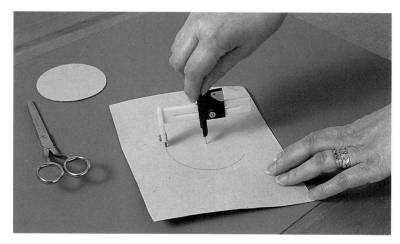

3 Set your compass to mark a 9cm (3½in) diameter circle on strong card. Cut around the circle to make a template.

4 Place the template on your material, and draw around it with a fine-tipped soft pencil or fine waterproof pen. You can fold the material and cut out two circles at once.

5 As a large quantity of material is needed for this project, cut out quite a few cotton circles at a time. (Keep the different colours and designs separate, perhaps in bags.) To use, you will need to fold each circle in half and then into four.

6 Work with the frame leaning at right angles to a table. Push a wooden knitting needle gently into the folded centre of a circle. Do not allow it to pierce the material.

7 Working from front to back and beginning in a corner, push the knitting needle and the tip of the circle about 1cm (½in) through the grey polyester.

8 On the reverse side, you will see little nodules of material.

9 Continue placing your circles about 2cm (¾in) apart, staggering them so that they slot snugly into each other. You do not have to work across – you can build up wherever you want your colours to go.

10 When you have completed a session, turn the frame over. Dip a plastic knife carefully into the latex – you only need to smear – and dab around each nodule to prevent them falling out. Be very meticulous in doing this. Then, just shake the frame gently to ensure all the nodules have been latexed.

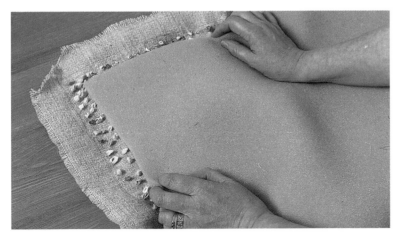

11 When you have completely covered the rug with cotton circles, remove from the frame. Place the finished rug right-side down on a table. Trim the material to about 7.5cm (3in) all around the rug. Place a piece of thin foam, the same size as the completed rug, on the reverse of the rug. This is to prevent the nodules from wearing out the backing.

12 Turn the surplus grey polyester down over the foam and, just catching the fabric on to the foam, tack all around, mitring the corners.

13 Cut the backing material slightly larger than the finished rug, and lay it over the foam, turning the edges under. Slip-stitch the backing to the rug, turning in the corners neatly (it is not necessary to mitre them). When this has been completed, back-stitch across the width of the rug at regular intervals, pushing the needle down through the backing and the foam and just catching it on the base material. You may hit some nodules which have been stiffened by the latex but just work around them.

SHAGGY BLUE RUG

ANN DAVIES

THE LOOM technique was rediscovered by the author in a long-out-of-print American book, and works on the principle of the oriental Ghiordes knot. The loom is simply built, or can be ordered from Ann Davies (see Suppliers on page 95). The loom is not a quick technique but it is one that can easily be picked up and put down. You can cut up strips, put them into a plastic bag, balance the loom on your knees and work away anywhere you happen to be!

Cotton does not lend itself to traditional hooking as it flattens and picks up the dirt easily, but it is usually the material that most people find readily available.

Using cotton and string makes this rug easily washable and therefore ideal for a bathroom or kitchen. Cushions for garden furniture could be made in the same way, and narrow strips of lurex might be knotted over fine string to make Christmas decorations.

62 × 40cm (24½ × 15¾in)

~

MATERIALS AND EQUIPMENT

- *loom* ● *hammer* ● *glue*
- *2 balls of string* ● *ballpoint pen* ● *ruler* ● *card at least 25 × 6.5cm (10 × 2½in)*
- *scissors* ● *cotton material*
- *strong thread* ● *needle*
- *thimble*

. . . . . .

1 The loom comes in kit form but is easily assembled. Put a ball of string over each dowel, as shown, and pull out enough string from each ball to reach across to the single dowel, with a little surplus.

2 Wrap each piece of string firmly around the nails at the top, winding it in a figure-of-eight so that it does not slip. As you do this, pull the ends down to the base of the loom so that they are taut.

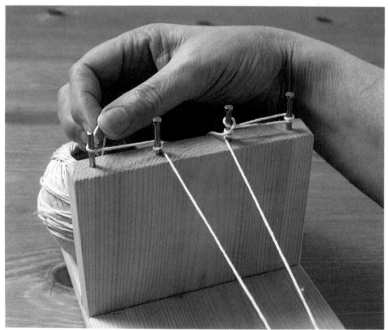

3 Bring the ends of the string down behind the single dowel and double-knot firmly.

4 Draw a rectangle at least 20cm (8in) long and 6.5cm (2½in) deep on a piece of firm card to use as a gauge when cutting the cotton. Cut out and fold in half, along the long edge.

5 Tear or cut the cotton on the straight into long strips 1cm (½in) wide.

6 Wrap a strip of material round and round the folded card in a single layer until either the card is covered or you have used up all your strip.

7 Insert your scissors into the centre of the folded card and cut through to make small strips of similar size.

8 Place one of these cut strips over the two strings about halfway down the loom.

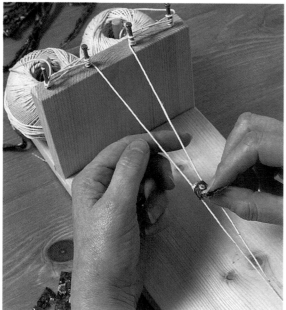

9 Bring the two ends up between the strings in front of the centre of the strip.

10 Holding the two ends firmly, pull the whole strip down to the single dowel. Continue working in this way until the string between the dowelling and the nails is fairly full.

11 Remove the 'full' area of string from the nails and bring it behind the dowel. Easing more string from the balls, wrap it around the nails until the new string between the dowel and the nails is taut as before. Continue making fabric strings in this way until you have a few feet of continuous knotted fabric.

The proportions of the oval rug in this project are determined by the length of the strip of knotted fabric. To work this out, subtract the desired finished width from the length of the centre strip. If you want a rug measuring, say, 81 × 61cm (32 × 24in), subtract 61 (24) from 81 (32) and make your centre strip 20cm (8in) long.

12 You may like to work for a while knotting the fabric and then do some coiling and sewing, before knotting some more fabric. The knotted fabric should be coiled clockwise in an oval or round shape and laced together on the back with strong linen thread. It is advisable to keep the knotted fabric flat on the table when you are sewing the coils together, easing the knotted fabric on the curves so that the rug will lie flat.

13 Do not cut the string until the rug is as large as you require. Then, tie the two strings in a knot and tuck into the pile.

'STAINED GLASS'

LANDSCAPE

ANN DAVIES

MANY PEOPLE associate rags with rug-making and don't realize that the technique can also be used to make other things such as pictures and wallhangings. The simply framed, small hooked picture shown here gives scope for using a variety of materials including tweeds, ribbons, knitting yarns, stretch fabrics and indeed anything else you have to hand. As you do not have to consider wear and tear, you can let your imagination take over when choosing the materials.

50 × 45cm (20 × 18in)

~

MATERIALS AND EQUIPMENT

● *61 × 56cm (24 × 22in) hessian/burlap* ● *2 × 61cm (24in) and 2 × 56cm (22in) artist's stretchers* ● *tracing paper* ● *design* ● *fine felt-tip pen* ● *transfer pencil* ● *dressmaker's pins* ● *iron* ● *staple gun and staples or drawing pins* ● *assortment of materials and yarns, including black material* ● *hook* ● *stapler remover or old screwdriver* ● *piece of hardboard, cut to finished size of design* ● *strong but not too thick string* ● *large-eyed needle* ● *thimble* ● *picture frame*

· · · · · ·

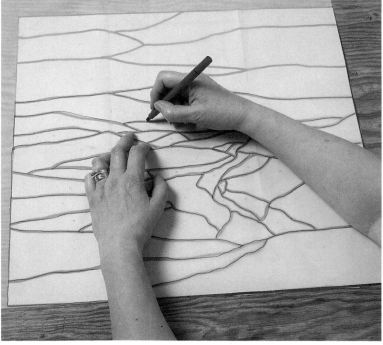

1 Ensure the edges of the hessian are straight when placed on the frame. Gently ease a thread from one edge of the hessian and pull it out – this will leave a line which can be used as a cutting guide.

2 Sketch your design and trace it on to tracing paper.

3 You will need to reverse the design when you transfer it on to the hessian. To do this, reverse the tracing paper and draw over the design again using a transfer pencil.

4 Pin the design down on the hessian with the transfer side face-down, ensuring that the design is straight and that the material is not distorted. Follow the lines of the design firmly with a hot iron, checking to make sure that all the lines are being transferred on to the hessian by lifting up a corner of the tracing paper gently. If, when you take the design off, you find some of the lines are faint, just go over them with felt-tip pen.

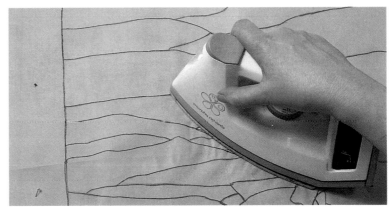

5 Assemble your frame. The piece of hessian must be large enough to cover the frame to its outside edge. You need to have a frame at least 10cm (4in) larger on all sides than the size of the picture. Attach the hessian to the frame using a staple gun or drawing pins. Begin by stapling two sides to make an L-shape, keeping the threads of the hessian straight; the edge of the frame acts as a guide. Then, stretching the hessian tightly, staple along the other two sides, using plenty of staples or drawing pins. Pay particular attention to the corners, bringing the staples right down to the edge.

6 Cut the black material into strips about 3mm (⅛in) wide, on the straight of the material. Working from the front, hook a single line of loops (see page 17) around all the outlines, including the edges. You should hook the outline slightly higher than the rest of the work so that the loops do not get lost in the pile when you fill in the remainder.

7 Fill in your design using a variety of materials that suggest fields, sunlight on corn, water, or similar landscape subjects.

8 You can see the design is building up. Here the sky is being hooked, using strips cut from a variety of woollens, worsteds, jersey and random-dyed cotton.

9 When you have finished hooking your picture, remove it from the frame. Cut the surplus hessian from around the picture, leaving a border of about 7.5cm (3in) on all sides, and trimming across the corners but not too closely.

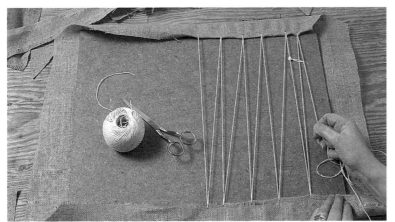

10 Place the hardboard squarely on the back of the picture, lining up with the edges of the design. Cut a long piece of string. Thread a large-eyed needle and make a knot at the other end of the string, then, turning the hessian under slightly to make a small hem (this stops the string from pulling the threads down), pull the string through until you reach the knot. Start at one end, just inside the corner of the picture, and lace from side to side. When you have used up the length of string, simply knot another length to it.

11 When you reach the edge, go back over the lacing to the other edge and repeat on the other two sides, paying particular attention to the corners. Take care that there is not too much hessian in the corners as this will make it difficult to frame. Finally, hang the picture in a suitable frame.

PRODDED DIAMOND RUG

CHRISTINE BIRCH

PRODDING, OR proggy, is one of the most traditional methods of rag rug-making; many people remember rag rugs being made in this way in the past.

As short pieces of material are used in this method, even more scraps are needed than for a hooked rug. Traditionally, a dark border would generally be prodded all around the rug, reflecting the predominant colours of the clothes people wore then. Today, prodded rugs show much more imagination in their subtle combination of colours and fabrics.

Because the pile of prodded rugs is shaggy, designs are not as clearly defined as in other methods, but this is part of the charm. This method can also be used for seat covers and cushions.

87 × 52cm (34¼ × 20½in)

~

MATERIALS AND EQUIPMENT

● *pencil* ● *graph or drawing paper* ● *ruler* ● *99 × 60cm (39 × 23½in) hessian/burlap or sacking* ● *fine and medium felt-tip pen* ● *sewing machine* ● *strong thread* ● *needle* ● *thimble* ● *frame with dowelling* ● *scissors* ● *assortment of materials* ● *prodder*

. . . . . .

1 Draw the diamond design on graph or drawing paper as a reference guide.

2 Outline the dimensions of your rug on a piece of hessian, using a fine felt-tip pen; mark the corners and then drag the pen through two threads to join up the marks or use a ruler as a guide. Mark the diamond shapes on the hessian with a thicker felt-tip pen.

3 Using a sewing machine, run a zigzag stitch all around the edge of the hessian to prevent it from fraying. Using strong thread, tack a hem on both of the shorter edges, wide enough to take the dowelling which will hold the hessian in the frame. Insert the dowelling.

4 Guide each length of dowelling into the channel of the top and bottom frame pieces.

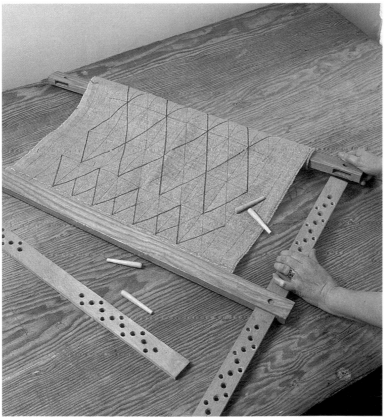

5 To make the work easier to handle, roll the surplus hessian over one edge of the frame; then push in the side pieces and stretch the hessian as tautly as possible.

6 Cut the chosen materials into pieces 2.5cm (1in) wide and 10cm (4in) long. You may prefer to do this piecemeal rather than cut up masses of small pieces all at once.

7 To remind you of where you
want the various colours of
your design to be, prod (see page
18) small pieces into the centre of
each diamond shape.

8 Continue prodding to fill in the
shapes outlined on the hessian.
Make distinctive borders between
the diamonds with a dark plain
colour if liked.

9 Remove the completed rug
from the frame, turn under the
surplus hessian to make a generous
hem on the reverse of the rug, and
slip-stitch down, being sure to
mitre and stitch down the corners.

SUPPLIERS

Weaving loom, traditional handmade hooks and proggies, hessian, grey polyester, transfer pencils, tuition, courses and lectures
Ann Davies, 1 Wingrad House, Jubilee Street, London E1 3BJ

Books on rug-making and associated crafts
Crafts of Quality Books, Unit 8, Bow Triangle Business Centre, Eleanor Street, London E3 4NP

Shuttle hooks and courses
Jenni Stuart Anderson, The Birches, Middleton-on-the-Hill, Herefordshire HR6 0H2

Shuttle hooks and large frame for shuttle hook work
Debbie Siniska, 12 Preston Court, The Crescent, Main Road, Sidcup, Kent DA15 6NT

Inexpensive rug canvas
Anita Fell, 'Secrets', off Whitehill Road, Crowborough, East Sussex TN6 1JA

Locker-needle hooks and tapestry canvas
Christine Ellis, Dolgellau Designs, Refail, Tir Stent Bach, Dolgellau, Gwynedd LL40 2RF

Locker-needle hooks
Maureen Preen, The Woodlands, Bron-y-Buckley, Welshpool, Powys SY21 7NQ

Out-of-print rug books
Keith Smith Books, 78b The Homend, Ledbury, Herefordshire

Pure new woollen material by the metre
Joshua Briggs & Sons Ltd., New Mills, Idle, Bradford

Artist's stretchers and PVA
Russell & Chapple, 23 Monmouth Street, London WC2H 9DD

Specialist frames as depicted in several of the projects
Christine Birch, Pen-yr-Allt Farm, Llanrhychwyn, Trefrew, Gwynedd LL27 0YX

Russell Dye System and other dyes
Carters, Station Road, Wickham Bishops, Essex CM8 3JB

For those interested in rag rug-making of all kinds, the Association of Rag Rug Makers produces a quarterly newsletter and will answer any queries or give advice on most aspects of rag rug-making other than weaving.
The Association of Rag Rug Makers, 1 Wingrad House, Jubilee Street, London E1 3BJ

Wool, plaiting aids, rug backings and foundations. Catalog $4.00
Braid Aid, 466 Washington Street, Pembroke, MA 92359

Supplies for all traditional hand hooking
Joan Moshimer's Rug Hooker Studio, Box 351, Kennebunkport, ME 04046

Unusual tools, backings and adhesive
Gloria E. Crouse, 4325 John Light Road N.E., Olympia, WA 98506

Linen backing material, dyes, cutters, frames, wool and hooks
Forestheart Studio, 21 South Carroll Street, Frederick, MD 21701

100% wool yardage and supplies
Ruth Ann's Wool, R.D. 4, Box 340, Muncha, PA 17756

Designs and supplies. Catalog $6.00
Rittermere-Hurst-Field, 45 Tyler Street, Box 487, Aurora, Ontario, L4G 3L6

INDEX

A

Anderson, Jenni Stuart, 67
Artist's stretchers, 9

B

Base and backing material, 12
    putting on frames, 16
Basic Techniques, 14–19
Birch, Christine, 92
Blossom Time, 73–77
Bright and Breezy, 67–71
Brin (see Hessian)
Broken Glass Rug, 43–47
Burlap (see Hessian)

C

Canvas, 12
Carpet binding, 12
Colours
    choosing, 14
Copts, 6
Cotton, 8
Crouse, Gloria, 73
Cushion Cover, 29–31

D

Davies, Ann, 29, 43, 73, 79, 85
Design
    considerations, 15
    transferring the, 16
    templates, 15
Dyeing, 15
Dyes, 12

E

Edge of the River, 61–65
Ellis, Christine, 61
Embroidery hoop, 35

F

Fell, Anita, 37
Frames,
    putting base material on, 16

G

Gallery, 21–28
Garden Wallhanging, 37–41
'Ghiordies' knot, 79

H

Hessian, 12
Hooking techniques, 17
Hooks
    latch, 12
    locker-needle, 12
    shuttle, 12

J

Jewellery, 33

K

Kent, William Winthrop, 6

L

Latch hook, 12
Lavender, 85
Locker-needle hook, 12
Loom techniques, 79, 80
Lucky Black Cat, 55–59

M

Macbeth, Ann, 6
Materials and Equipment, 8–13
Materials
    base and backing, 12
    range of, 8–9

P

Polyester, 12
Prodded Diamond Rug, 91–94
Prodders, 12
Prodding techniques, 12
Proggy, 93

R

Rag rugs
    braided (see plaited)
    history of, 6, 7
    hooked, 6, 7
    plaited, 7
    prodded, 6, 7
Razzle Dazzle, 33–55
Reakes, Lizzie, 33, 49

S

Shaggy Blue Rug, 79–83
Shuttle hook, 12
Siniska, Debbie, 55
Stained Glass Landscape, 85–89
Star-burst Rug, 49–53
Strips
    making, 14
Suppliers, 95

T

Techniques
    base material, putting on a
        frame, 16
    colours, choosing, 14
    design, transferring the, 17
    hooking, 17
    loom, 79, 80
    strips, making, 14
    prodding, 18
Templates, 15, 16

V

Vikings, 6

W

Wool fabrics, 8